EAGLE CLAWS
FOR FREEDOMS
Cause

(A COLLECTION OF AMERICAN POEMS ON DRAINING THE SWAMP)
HINT: MASK NOT REQUIRED.)

To order additional copies of this book, contact:
Xlibris
844-714-8691
www.Xlibris.com
Orders@Xlibris.com

ISBN: 978-1-6641-5554-1 (sc)
ISBN: 978-1-6641-5553-4 (e)

Print information available on the last page

Rev. date: 01/29/2021

INTRODUCTION

"EAGLE CLAWS FOR FREEDOM'S CAUSE" is a sometimes humorous sometimes serious look at America. Her past her present & her future.

DeAnna Lorraine who ran for Congress in San Francisco in 2020 is the person who most of the poems in this book are about. A successful author in her own right she has written two books (Making Love Great Again & more recently Taking Back America). She has been a champion for conservative thought. Particularly raising awareness against the evils of modern day Feminism.

Although her run did not end with victory at the ballot box. In the process her's became a leading voice in the upswell of conservatism which began to reassert itself again in America in the year 2016. With its influence continuing to grow long into the future.

DeAnna has had the honor of being retweeted on six separate occasions by the President of the United States. (TRUMP) You can find her on various social media platforms these days. (At least the ones that still allow uncensored speech.) Her unorthodox (energetic) campaign & engaging personality became the inspiration for most of the poems in this book.

She is currently on hiatus from hosting her own news show on Infowars. Keeping herself active organizing & attending rallies across the United States. As of this writing I have not yet had the distinct pleasure of meeting her personally but Lord willing I very much look forward to doing so in the near future.

The rest of the book contains poems drawing parallels in America from from 1776 to the present. With the events beginning in 2016 the unexpected (by many) NOT ME election of President Donald Trump. This cataclysmic event signifying the restoration of America's rightful place as the world's leading beacon of hope for the freedom of man on this planet called earth.

1776

· ·

America was founded & built upon the pioneering spirit of rugged individualism. At no time since 1776 has that spirit been as threatened as it is today. In keeping with the traditions of the signing of the Declaration of Independence. My motto/challenge for America this year is. "IF YOU WEAR A MASK YOUR NOT UP TO ITS TASK".

I would gladly affix my John Hancock to the declaration if they want to add it in as a special clause (just for this year). I believe Thomas Jefferson & Benjamin Franklin would be pleased. What say you?

DeAnna to Florida

Let me tell you about the girl who came via California way who goes by the name of DEANNA: Her relocation to Florida is like a gift of heavenly sent MANNA:

The sound of her laughter is so wondrously INTOXICATING: It's time to do some CELEBRATING:

Don't ask her to wear a MASK: If you want your good health to LAST: Delta wants to ban her from FLIGHT: She told them instead to go fly a KITE:

She gives it to the left honest & STRAIGHT: It's this candor that they HATE:

Her smile shines so BRIGHT: It could only come from a lady who's RIGHT:

So here's to a warm welcome to HURRICANE DeAnna LORRAINE: Florida will never ever be the SAME

I REALLY WANNA WANNA MEET DEANNA

DeAnna marches to the beat of her own DRUM: Her end goal is to avoid the USA from turning into a third world SLUM: She did more than her part making an office RUN: To throw out all the swamp SCUM:

I write poems just for FUN: They do not need a bass to pick or a guitar to STRUM: The kit of her DRUMS: Provide more than enough section for the RHYTHM: And if you like to sing you can also HUM: I REALLY WANNA WANNA MEET DEANNA:

We could have a "reel" fishing BLAST: By trolling the ocean's bottom or throwing out a live baited CAST: If the seas are to rough to leave PORT: WE could always try another SPORT: With time to SHARE: We could roll a ball down the bowling alley lane looking to score a strike not a pin SPARED:

It would be an evening filled with the endless POSSIBILITIES: That could only happen with FROLICKY UNPREDICTABILITY: I REALLY WANNA WANNA MEET DEANNA:

If bowling is not the tea she prefers in her CUP: We could study the bible for good LUCK: If we stand on holy GROUND: We will ably make decisions that are sure to be SOUND: I REALLY WANNA WANNA MEET DEANNA:

I have been zoned a platonic FRIEND: It's true but hard to COMPREHEND: I've promised her my behavior would always be GENTLEMANLY: A hallmark of true MASCULINITY: So there is no need for pretense or make PRETEND: I REALLY WANNA WANNA MEET DEANNA

DEANNA IS NOT A QUITER

DeAnna LORRAINE makes Deep Staters hang their heads in SHAME: Tune into her SHOW to stay in the KNOW:

She has the SCOOP to keep you in the LOOP:

Who knows she may even sing a song or TWO it's hard to believe but it's TRUE:

They tried to silence her voice by banning her from TWITTER: Little did they know that won't WORK because they're such JERKS & she's not a QUITTER:

So for the best coverage of the Trump CAMPAIGN: Listen in on infowars to DeAnna LORRAINE: That way on election night you won't have anyone to BLAME: Instead you will be able to enjoy a glass of celebratory CHAMPAGNE:

POEM NOEM

If you want to get the right SCORE: Without longing for MORE: Tune in to DeAnna Lorraine on INFOWARS:

DeAnna gives the news from her heart STRAIGHT: So you don't have to worry about it's being FAKE:

She makes this sacrifice for the FOLKS: In the hopes they will get WOKE:

DeAnna LORRAINE voluntarily puts herself in harm's WAY: Because she sincerely believes in what she has to SAY: Those who care about her can show their concern by bending their knee to PRAY: You see she is not one to frivolously COMPLAIN: How many of us can make such a CLAIM:

Of course it's not something everyone would DO: Let's be grateful for people like her who are willing TOO:

I believe she feels it her duty as a great American CITIZEN: To make her country a better place to live IN:

Recently she got us a story from a place called the blind PIG: Where unsuspecting patrons go for a drink a dance or a SWIG.

Dancing to the music was DISAVOWED: Now is not the time to follow that CROWD: We voice our displeasure by telling the SWINE (oink oink) dancing in public is not a CRIME: So go ahead & give me a FINE: From me they'll never see another DIME.

If you want your news delivered with humor beauty & BRAINS: Get it EXPLAINED to you by watching DeAnna LORRAINE: As she brings the left PAIN leaving them with nothing but an aching MIGRAINE

DeAnna I am glad you like my POEM just remember it was written for you not Kristi NOEM:

I'm not sure what on election evening will be more COMPELLING: Trump's WINNING: DeAnna Lorraine's SINGING or Joe Biden's attempted election RIGGING

POEM NOEM 2

It is said that man can not live by bread alone (or FRADULENT election results) for that matter:

DeAnna now is the time history has chosen for us to destroy the deep state once & for all. How great is it going to be for the COUNTRY when all is revealed that the man who tried to steal the PRESIDENCY (Allegedly) will spend the rest of his life in a FEDERAL PENITENTIARY:

Big tech is also on the clock too: TWITTER is just a fancy word for LITTER It won't be long before they get flushed down the SHITTER:

We are also tired of being SCREWED by you TUBE: They better get in LINE because they are not far BEHIND:

BANANA REPUBLIC

Banana republics are full of problems FRAUGHT: Join infowars this Saturday in D.C. to expose election FRAUD:

Though infowars is BANNED: By most antisocial media don't be conned into THINKING to take a STAND they are UNWILLING:

FOR the love of this LAND: All of us citizens can do their part by lending them a HAND in joining them in the Stop the Steal CARAVAN:

Yea they have had their share of TRAVAILS: But have no doubt in this fight they will PREVAIL: Media slimy politicians & their ilk are sorely MISTAKEN if they believe infowars is going to sit passively by & allow this election to be TAKEN:

This time they have an ace up their SLEEVE: Who not even Nancy Pelosi could DECEIVE:

Her name is DeANNA LORRAINE: She will be on hand to set the record STRAIGHT: In her quest to make America GREAT:

The forecast is calling for little to no RAIN: So come be ENTERTAINED by all of the gang especially DeAnna LORRAINE: You will be really glad you CAME!

INDIANA

Indiana there is something to SEE: Indiana the land of basketball & Sycamore TREES:

Indiana lies midwestern values that belie her California ROOTS: Indiana lies rugged individualism which she proudly wears on her newly minted cowboy BOOTS:

Indiana you can find your piece of AMERICANA: Whether it be a house or a CABANA:

Indiana lies a share of the American DREAM: Indiana there is no in BETWEEN:

Indiana lies an outgoing personality for all to SEE: Indiana lies her values of Family God & Country:

Indiana is really pretty on the surface & easy to look AT: But her real beauty lies on her inside imagine THAT:

Indiana lies a force for GOOD: In spite of all the slings & arrows she has WITHSTOOD:

Indiana lies a real Tesoriero (that's treasure for our non-european friends) to APPRECIATE: Indiana lies America's favorite State!

DEANNA IN ATLANTA

In 1864 in his famous march to the sea which began in Atlanta Union General Techumsah Sherman promised to "Make Georgia Howl"

Today there is a new General in town. DeAnna LORRAINE of infowars FAME: Looking to make Georgia's election fraudsters throw in the TOWEL:

DeAnna will be in ATLANTA: To squelch the STORM that will make dirty politicians SQUEAL if they refuse to CONFORM. They would be better off trying to make a DEAL: Before she forces them to stop the STEAL:

General Lorraine marches in with nothing but her stars & STRIPES: But anyone who knows her knows she will make the scammers run with FRIGHT:

In Georgia it's PEACHES with cobbler & CREAM: That helps in finding ballots UNSEEN:

And just like Sherman's march to the sea: Georgia will howl from ATLANTA to SAVANNAH: All because: DEANNA was in ATLANTA.

P.S. Here is a Thanksgiving joke for YOU whenever your feeling BLUE:
What's the difference between a Turkey & a Democrat? One is full of stuffing the other full of Turkey droppings! GOBBLE GOBBLE GOBBLE
8
Thanksgiving Leftovers

DEANNA CAN BE CERTAIN

As the Turkey trot now gives way to Reindeer games this holiday season: Many are a little WEARY: In hindsight the events of the year 2020 will have been proven necessary to be able to be seen more CLEARLY: Focus behind the ironies CURTAIN: Of her fate DeAnna can be CERTAIN:

I wish it were not so but DeAnna is HURTIN: She is forging a path all her OWN: Which at times leaves her feeling vulnerable & ALONE: But alas nary a doubt. Of her convictions DeAnna will neither be unbound nor BROKEN: Of this DeAnna can be CERTAIN:

It was Jesus who proclaimed a prophet UNKNOWN in their own HOME Regardless of whatever contradictory evidence SHOWN: For her adherence to principle. Her feet shall be washed her spirit cleansed Someday she will be ATONED: Of this DeAnna can be Certain:

Her pains & ACHES are all to REAL brought on in large part by a news media used as a SHIELD: For evil actors who refuse to YIELD: To them we will not SUCCUMB: Their hour of reckoning has COME: IT won't be long until once again families can become ONE: Of this DeAnna can be Certain:

Although she is still FREE (INEXPLICABLY): She has never really shown much interest in getting to know ME: And that's ok! As long as she likes my POETRY: Of this DeAnna can be Certain:

DEANNA'S GIFT

It has been said the best things in life are FREE: So what will be DeAnna's gift left this year under her Christmas TREE:

When DeAnna wakes up on Christmas morning if it were up to ME: She would find her gift to be the nurturing touch of her FAMILY:

Because of Covid FEAR unfortunately that will not be happening this YEAR: So what will DeAnna's gift be?

It will not REPLACE: The loving EMBRACE or sight of seeing a longed for relatives FACE: But for this year (and prayerfully this year only) this poem will serve as the GIFT that gives her heart & soul a LIFT:

This Merry Christmas when Santa arrives in DeAnna's TOWN: I hope she will be able to muster a smile not a FROWN:

It has to be painful to ENDURE: Feelings so uncertain so UNSURE:

But you see unlike years past under her evergreen will not be the usual gifts of stocking stuffers & candy canes. And while it won't be as much fun as frolicking & singing Christmas JINGLES with her family to MINGLE: DeAnna's gift this year is much more sincere: That could not even be delivered by ole Kris KRINGLE:

You see in this year of Covid. DeAnna's gift is of a soul that's FREE: To be whoever God wants it to BE: This is DeAnna's gift.

D.C. DEANNA

As the restorative war of 2020 rolls on the field of battle is not the wheatfields of Gettysburg nor the river of Washington's Delaware crossing. The uniforms are not blue & GRAY: Blue jeans, t-shirts, & sneakers are more apropos in America TODAY:

The swampy streets of D.C. is where all citizen soldiers need to BE: D.C. DeAnna will be there leading the charge in the FLESH: Her appearance is importantly VITAL: For our national SURVIVAL: The supreme court of the land would not ACQUIESCE: To a challenge put forth by a coalition of States with the HOPES: Of protecting themselves from fraudulent VOTES: D.C. DeANNA is making the case for the court to have a look SEE: Otherwise citizens will not have any confidence in election INTEGRITY: Make no mistake this election if not certified LEGALLY: Will forever alter our nation's SOVEREIGNTY:

The courts can sometimes be ruled without any ACCOUNTABILITY: Which can lead to rulings that run counter to freedom & LIBERTY: This is the MANTRA of D.C. DEANNA:

D.C. DeAnna makes the case through the bullhorn LOUDLY: Standing behind her public declarations so unapologetically PROUDLY: The capital city of D.C is the only place where this can be done PROPERLY: D.C. DEANNA knows if she does not charge ON: Soon our republic will be GONE: It will have more in common with commie HAVANA: Than the big blue beautiful skies of MONTANA:

D.C. DeAnna's weaponry of choice is not the staff of a shepherd, a soldiers musket or a spartan's SPEAR: Just an unshakeable ZEAL: Combined with an unmistakable sex APPEAL:

There are many other things D.C. DeAnna could be DOIN: Like any HEROINE she chooses to save her country from RUIN:

With D.C. DeAnna we realize how we are truly BLESSED: With D.C. DeAnna no one should want to MESS:

MONTANA STATE CAPITOL BVILDING.

DEANNA'S YEARLY DIVINE

It was almost a year ago to the day DeAnna came into my VIEW: An inspired run for Congress being her PURVIEW: I have tried to support her ever SINCE: Because I knew in word or in deed she does not MINCE:

From the deep rooted TREE: Of Governmental HIERARCHY: A Lot of apples ROTTEN: Resisted her calls to help the DOWNTRODDEN: If she runs again lessons cherished & learned will not have been FORGOTTEN:

People in the HOOD: Liked her because they knew where she STOOD: DeAnna not only did CARE: She actually put her action where her time was by visiting them THERE: People she was trying to serve knew how to spot a PHONY: All they have ever been fed by other politicians are lines full of BALONEY:

DeAnna even did something none of the other politicians DID: She ended her tireless campaign by contracting COVID:

Maybe this had something to do in her determination to PURSUE: About Covid all that was false or TRUE:

"Film your HOSPITAL": Proceeded to go VIRAL: Causing an UPROAR: That still makes a lot of uppity people SORE: The intensity of the BLOWBACK would have made a lesser person CRACK: DeAnna even sent me a text thanking me for always having her BACK:

DeAnna also had a rift with CARDI B: Who only has one item to SELL: And believe me it probably ain't all that SWELL: Anyway who is SHE:

DeAnna has now left her native California pastures for grasses GREENER: She even has a show of her OWN: And calls Texas HOME: But it has not changed her DEMEANOR:

She feels a lot of CONSTERNATION about the goings on in our NATION: Who knows if you are LUCKY: You may even get to meet her at a RALLY:

There is no quit in DeAnna: Her ascension to the queen's THRONE: Has not been ended only POSTPONED:

So before you GO: Call into her infowars SHOW: Or stop by & say HELLO: With her you will always learn something you did not already KNOW:

REVOLUTION

Remember the song Revolution by the Beatles:

"If you go carrying pictures of Chairman MAO: You ain't gonna make it with anyone ANYHOW:

Considering the alleged election interference by the Chinese this years refrain is:

"If you go carrying ballots marked by President XI: There will be a lot of angry Americans who DISAGREE:

HEAR YE HEAR YE

DID BIDEN REALLY WIN? OR IS IT THE LATEST ELABORATE HOAX PERPETRATED ON THE FOLKS

He has always been a DOLT: Even before dementia took it's HOLD: A gaffe machine extraordinaire ready with an ill advised quip or QUOTE: One of the many reasons why 80 million citizens are at a hat of a drop's moment's NOTE: READY to REVOLT: To believe he got more votes than Trump go down as history's longest running JOKE:

Previous runs for the highest office in the land were met with a big ole DUD: When allegations of copying speeches surfaced his campaigns fizzled like 4th of July fireworks stuck in the MUD:

For some inexplicable reason he was the one chosen to do the bidding for the LEFT: We know of any logical reasoning they are BEREFT: Allegations of election fraud once again gives our country a big problem to solve in this alleged election THEFT:

There are many many tremendous American Patriots sounding the ALARM: (ring ring ring) In the spirit of Paul Revere's midnight ride (THE COVID IS COMING THE COVID IS COMING) to thwart the left's efforts to do America any more HARM: Rudy Jenna Sidney & LIN (to name a few) are stretching themselves THIN: Burning the midnight OIL: In the effort to SPOIL: THE dastardly plots FOIL:

They once tried the IMPOSITION: Of PROHIBITION: The People did not LISTEN: Now as then they tried to steal the people's FUN: But failed in getting the job DONE: The people rose up & WON:

As in any rebellion whether it BE: WHISKEY Boxer or TEA: There are many odd turns with twists of plots THICKENING: Filled with booby trapped roadblocks on the path to WINNING: Just like the rebellion of 1776 modern eagle's soar by staying focused on the GOAL: Of winning back the election that was all but STOLE: (Allegedly)

Some have advised putting a pause on MAGA. With no institutional help coming Trump's WAY: He should step aside to fight another DAY: To those I say not only is that FOOLHARDY: IF MAGA admits DEFEAT: By going into a misguided RETREAT: Come 2024 it will be to TARDY: To take back whatever might be left of our tattered PARTY:

From its INCEPTION: MAGA forged ahead of its own accord regardless of those who had their legitimate MISCONCEPTIONS: Their fears were quickly ERASED: When looking at MAGA's accomplishments on values together FACED:

Those with selfish AMBITIONS: Instead of being idiots useful should spend more time in self REFLECTION: MAGA has always been very INCLUSIVE: Ask all the millions it lifts & INFUSSES:

Over the objections of the traitors in our MIDST: Whose sole mission in life is only to RESIST: The chaos at the southern BORDER: Quickly turned from free for all to law & ORDER:

American farmers once again began to make "HAY": When all the cash flow going to China was rerouted back their WAY. Car makers also returned bringing back JOBS: Allowing manufacturers to afford the farmers corn on the COB:

Peace long sought a PRIZE: Suddenly began to RISE: Much to everyone's SURPRISE: North Korea a longtime prickly thorn in everybody's SIDE: Came to the table for peace no longer with nuclear ambitions to HIDE:

Even the middle east. Always known for its PROCLIVITY: TO endless HOSTILITY: Has now committed to an easing of generational TENSIONS: It's difficult to believe this truce would have happened without serious MAGA MEDIATION: Israel America's truest friend in the region without RESERVATION: Had to be pleased America finally made Jerusalem the base of it's embassy RECOGNITION:

As the earth turns around its ORBIT: All the good things MAGA has done risk going unnoticed if fake news is unwilling to report IT.

Ahead lie many frontiers as of yet not TACKLED: The pandemic for one of which we want to be UNSHACKLED: Swamp draining needs to be a PRIORITY: To restore our nation's GLORY:

The global reset needs to be quickly UNDONE: If the American nation is remain a sovereign ONE:

There are many other things in the futures STORE: But they have to be done now they can not wait to be restored in 2024:

HIGH OCTANE DEANNA LORRAINE

There is nothing she likes to do More: Other than host her show on INFOWARS: To the station she has made great SACRIFICE: By her they need do right nothing less will SUFFICE:

I dearly miss her podcasts. It offered the audience a personal TOUCH: That always means so MUCH:

She is high OCTANE: DeAnna LORRAINE:

Put the camera lens on ZOOM: Your heart like a car at INDY will start racing VOOM VOOM VOOM:

She is understandably sad this CHRISTMAS: Suffering from a bout of HOMESICKNESS:

To get her through it I will HELP: The first Noel the angels did SING: I offer her my prayer & a WING:

Merry Christmas to High Octane DeAnna Lorraine

CHRISTMAS 2020

I could write about her FOREVER: In sleet snow or shine through all kinds of Christmas WEATHER: From Los Angeles to MAINE: There is something so special about DeANNA LORRAINE: Although I have as yet not met HER:

We'll work on that in twenty twenty ONE: It will surely be so much FUN: We can share a toast of good CHEER: With a tall glass of BEER:

In Christmas 2020 she might be feeling down in the DUMP: Believing her stocking a coal of LUMP: Bethlehem's promised STAR: Seemingly unusually FAR:

But for DeAnna LORRAINE: My star will never WANE: It burns bright by the candlelight on the window PANE:

When Santa comes down the chimney with CARE: I wish I could be standing THERE:

Ask him to give his Reindeer a break from the weatherly Fog: Share a cup of egg's NOG: Courtesy of his jolly ole friend BOB: (HO HO HO)

Santa DeAnna & I would share in a prayer DIVINE: Under the Christmas PINE:

For the baby tucked away in a manger shivering in the COLD: For whom wise men brought gifts of GOLD: To fulfill the promise of Christmas 2020 & like any other to HOLD: In celebration of the greatest story ever TOLD:

Twitter TADDER Pitter PADDER: Why is it important & why should it MATTER: 2020 being in the BOOK: Is back where we really want to LOOK: INSTEAD: We are better served looking AHEAD: 2021 can be the year of deep state SHATTER:

Digital SOLDIERS: Public opinion MOULDERS: We carry our nation's fate on our SHOULDERS:

Forget the courts of KANGAROO: Or the elaborately staged COUP: America is a country ruled by the ordinary many not the elite FEW: With every right to ask the why what & how from the WHO.

We are called to be America's standard BEARERS: Not oversee her demise as it's PALLBEARERS:

2021 can be remembered the year that made wearing a MASK: A relic of America's revolutionary PAST: Bad times like good being made to never LAST: With this is what history has us TASKED:

It will take a yeoman's effort to get this job DONE: Like in colonial times the red white & blue do not from a challenge RUN: From the PRESIDENT: To every day RESIDENT: On DOWN: From America's largest cities to the most rural of it's TOWNS:

Vaccines Masks & Lockdowns are not the American way in any era Old or NEW: An uncivil imposition on citizens UNDUE: People pushing mandates need to be shown a CLUE: We are free Americans with many differing points of VIEW: Exercising our god given rights whenever we want TO:

We will take our country BACK: Without any courage LACKED: Like 1776 we will once again ring liberty's BELL: To mandates & lockdowns bid adieu & FAREWELL: A miraculous story for our grandchildren to TELL:

Some may ask why all the FUSS: The answer is something to do we MUST: If we are to live up to the motto in god we TRUST:

We will answer historys call for better not WORSE: By turning 2021 into a blessing from 2020's CURSE:

Forefathers will be made proud for once not being spun in a GRAVE: Proudly looking down from ABOVE: With a reverent parent to child LOVE: Knowing that the road of freedom they fought so hard on cobblestoned bricks to PAVE: Was just as they envisioned by ordinary citizens SAVED:

LORRAINE'S ARMY

Robert E. LEE once commandeered the Army of Northern Virginia: His no match for Lorraine's ARMY INSIGNIA:

Rough riders from Texas CENTRAL: In the RV: On the way to D.C.: To meet others from around the COUNTRY: The cause for the republic salvation ESSENTIAL:

Cancel the coup they WILL: It's a country free STILL:

Leader Lorraine adorned in feminine's PINK: More beautiful than a springs Virginia Rose in BLOOM: Saves our country from impending DOOM: Rallying her fellow countrymen to twice THINK: Rising them to historic challenge not SHRINK:

Valiantly willing to brave the shivers COLD: (brrrrrrr) Like battle hardened warriors of OLD: LORRAINE & her compatriots by night & day TRAVEL: To our nation's CAPITAL: In determination of who STOLE:

Traitors be DAMMED: We are on to their SCAM: Damn the torpedoes batten down the HATCHES: Then watch as the planned coup CRASHES:

From the home of the BRAVE: Their efforts worthy of PRAISE:

Our country sufficed under the GALLANTRY: Of Lorraine's ARMY CAVALRY: Taking the cause to the road in the SOUPED up RV:........ OF THEE I SING.....

ASSORTED JOKES QUOTES & SAYINGS FROM THE CAMPAIGN OF DEANNA LORRAINE

That's our girl DeAnna Lorraine at a "walkaway" march rally yesterday. Does she look GREAT or what. Now they're going to have to make temperature checks mandatory all over California if they don't already. WOWZA!

"TAKING BACK AMERICA" (Fighting Pelosi & Amazon) How you can win without wearing a mask!

FIGHTING NANCY PELOSI (and the swamp) Does not entitle you to a $14 pint of ice cream!

Politicians in San Francisco are going to need some extra rolaids when this book comes out!

Fire up the grill & get it READY. Tonight begins the road to 2020...not to worry Trump will bring the SIZZLE: From rare to well DONE: Trump will be sure to bring the FUN...Polls are for FOOLS: Don't be a TOOL: Trump brings the SIZZLE: BIDEN the SIZZLE:

Our Country is in fine shape with that crew of Patriots on board & at the helm: Just one request though. Can you save me some of those Hor Dourves!

That's a nice picture. Those colors contrast against each other perfectly. Then of course you've got those big baby blues. AY YAY YAY!

Lincoln gave us the Emancipation Proclamation. With a tweet Trump just gave the NFL the Emasculation Proclamation.

Those horses are very majestic looking. I'm going to need a new sport on Sunday's. Maybe I'll take up Polo!

Fishermen & Politicians have something in common. They both love to tell tales.

Whoever is Deep State practicing voodoo is going to find themselves in deep doo doo.

Trump 2020 in the land of good & PLENTY: People who vote Trump there will be so MANY: For Biden hardy ANY: He's so weak Trump will win the Presidency without having spent a PENNY:

DeAnna whatever you order at the restaurant. I hope it pisses the vegetarians off.

CLOSING PRAYER

I pray that God continues to bless the United States of America with his hand DIVINE: In the name of freedom for all of MANKIND:

America was founded as freedom's first frontier let's pray the sun has not yet set on the "great experiment" on EARTH: It is here I pray that GOD allow again the sun to rise on freedom with a new BIRTH: Let it to prosper & flourish: Protecting its precious WORTH:

I pray for godly INSPIRATION: As well as heavenly PROTECTION: For the PEOPLE: Engaged in fighting against that which is not born of GOD: So they can successfully finish the called upon JOB:

The Lord's calling awaits us ALL: Opening your heart to HIM: Will make miraculous changes WITHIN: God answers the day or night CALL: I pray anyone reading this prayer will stand TALL: In the name of God: There is fruitful opportunity not a need to STALL:

In the holy name of Jesus RESURRECTION: I Pray for healing in our land & all it's individuals.

AMEN

LIGHT

In the beginning God said "LET THERE BE LIGHT": He did not distinguish between left or RIGHT:

Eve tempted a bite from the APPLE: Put in motion the temptations of which man has ever since had to GRAPPLE:

When out on the ocean waves CALM: God's goodness holds the answers in the hands PALM:

Sun set or RISE: Tide lows or HIGHS: No need to squint or a look STRAINED: You can easily see the light's beam God placed inside DeAnna LORRAINE: To combat so many LIES: In the whites of her EYES:

ABOUT THE AUTHOR

One day seemingly out of nowhere the inspiration to write a book of poetry came to me. I never fancied myself a poet. It was not something long planned. I have always enjoyed writing (mostly about sports & the outdoors) when I had accumulated a certain number of poems. I thought why not put them into a book. Especially at such a critical time in America's history. What's happening in America is very personal to me. My family had to flee the evils of communism from Cuba. The stories of which left an everlasting impression. I was raised in Pennsylvania & now live in Florida. Where I enjoy deep sea fishing & scuba diving.

Closing Summary:

The election of 2021 if nothing else brought America to it's BRINK: A time which made many not just in America but around the world not just question but also for the first time THINK: No longer simply partake of a kool aid DRINK:

Where we go from here no one as of yet KNOWS: But shapely events most definitely have millions of citizens aroused and on their TOES:

The goal for MAGA remains the SAME: For the light of truth to finally meet the light of day lies and darkness no longer being tolerated as a GAME: For swampy political GAIN:

MAGA is here to stay people by the millions AWAKE: Those that aren't yet know it is also your liberty at STAKE: MAGA will always advocate for the human CONDITION: By just as in 1776 restoring our republic to it's constitutional MISSION:

ACKNOWLEDGEMENTS

I want to thank my parents, my sister, & my friends Bill Eacrett & Ron Gay whose humor is always indespensible.

Pastor Greg Young for the prayerful inspiration.

My mother was an incredible listening board.

I would like to thank DeAnna Lorraine whose run for Congress & tireless efforts to help restore America to her original glory were the inspiration for this book.

America would be very lucky to have 330 million DeAnna Lorraine's by her side. But I will settle for just having one in Congress. Then I could rest easy.

Printed in the United States
By Bookmasters